AMAZING MACHINES

BULLDOZERS

BY QUINN M. ARNOLD

CREATIVE EDUCATION • CREATIVE PAPERBACKS

Published by Creative Education and Creative Paperbacks
P.O. Box 227, Mankato, Minnesota 56002
Creative Education and Creative Paperbacks are imprints of
The Creative Company
www.thecreativecompany.us

Design by The Design Lab
Production by Chelsey Luther
Art direction by Rita Marshall
Printed in the United States of America

Photographs by Alamy (Dino Fracchia, Rosanne Tackaberry),
Dreamstime (Agg), Getty Images (J. Ronald Lee, Joel Sartore,
wesvandinter), iStockphoto (AMA66, filonmar, Pro-syanov), Shut-
terstock (artiomp, JVrublevskaya, rtem, Vladimir Sazonov)

Library of Congress Cataloging-in-Publication Data
Names: Arnold, Quinn M., author.
Title: Bulldozers / Quinn M. Arnold.
Series: Amazing machines.
Includes bibliographical references and index.
Summary: A basic exploration of the parts, variations, and
worksites of bulldozers, the leveling and scraping machines. Also
included is a pictorial diagram of variations of bulldozers.
Identifiers: ISBN 978-1-60818-886-4 (hardcover) / ISBN 978-1-
62832-502-7 (pbk) / ISBN 978-1-56660-938-8 (eBook)
This title has been submitted for CIP processing under LCCN
2017937610.

CCSS: RI.1.1, 2, 4, 5, 6, 7; RI.2.2, 5, 6, 7, 10; RI.3.1, 5, 7, 8;
RF.1.1, 3, 4; RF.2.3, 4

First Edition HC 9 8 7 6 5 4 3 2 1
First Edition PBK 9 8 7 6 5 4 3 2 1

Table of Contents

Bulldozers are heavy

machines. They have strong steel blades.
Flat blades were first used more than 100
years ago. Farm animals pulled them
through fields. By the 1920s, the blades
were put on tractors. They cleared forests
and fields alike.

The body of a bulldozer is still called the tractor today.

Bulldozer blades can be specially made to do certain jobs.

There are three kinds of bulldozer blades. Straight bulldozer blades are the shortest. Universal blades are tall and curved. Their wide **side wings** keep things in front of the blade. Combination blades are shorter than universal blades. They have smaller side wings.

side wings the flat parts at each end of the blade; these keep material in front of the blade

The biggest bulldozers carve away the earth at surface mines.

Straight blades are often used for **grading** roads and land. Universal blades move a lot of loose dirt or sand. Heavy-duty jobs call for a combination blade. These blades push heavy rocks in **quarries**.

grading smoothing a surface

quarries large pits from which rocks, stone, or other building materials are dug out

Small bulldozer blades are about five feet (1.5 m) wide. The biggest bulldozers can have blades more than 30 feet (9.1 m) wide. They can push heavier loads. But they need more room to move around.

Small bulldozers are also known as mini dozers.

Large bulldozers often have a ripper. This is on the back of the machine. The bulldozer drags the giant claw behind it. The ripper tears into hard ground. It digs up stumps.

Rippers are common in mines and quarries, where they break up rocks.

Caterpillar treads are made of thick rubber or strong steel.

A bulldozer moves on **caterpillar treads**. These grip the land. They spread out the bulldozer's weight. This keeps the heavy machine from sinking into soft spots. A bulldozer can help pull other machines that get stuck.

caterpillar treads bands looped around roller wheels to help heavy vehicles move

Farmers and construction crews bulldoze trees and small buildings. They remove rocks and stumps. A rake attachment clears brush.

Farmers may use dozers to clear land for new fields.

Bulldozers help make roads. Sharp blades shave the ground. They spread dirt and dig ditches. At landfills, bulldozers crush trash. At mines, they push large rocks.

Spiked wheels help bulldozers crush trash at some landfills.

Bulldozers work hard

in many different places. Look for these

powerful pushers at a worksite near you!

*Bulldozers with treads
cannot drive on paved
roads.*

Bulldozer Blueprint

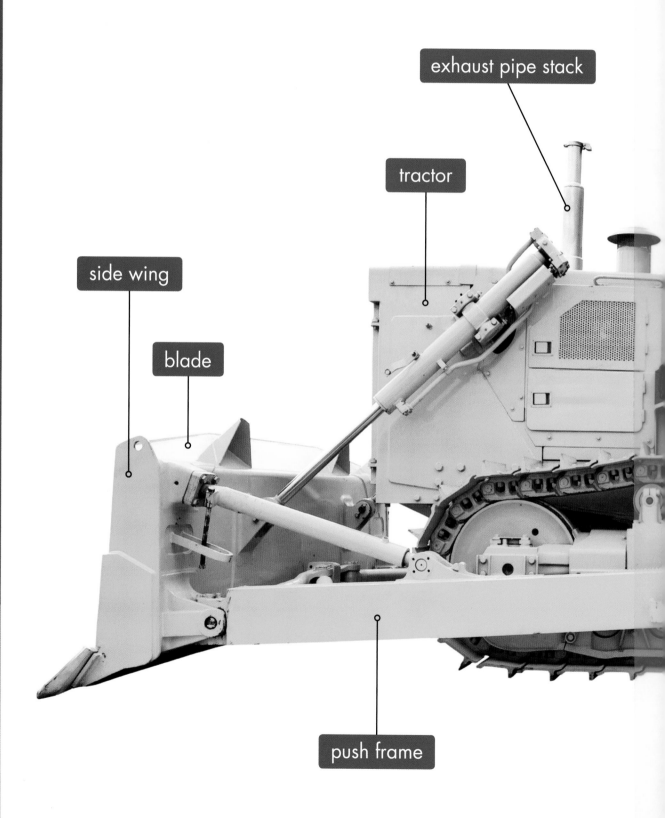

exhaust pipe stack

tractor

side wing

blade

push frame

cab

ripper

tread

Read More

Bowman, Chris. *Monster Bulldozers*. Minneapolis: Bellwether Media, 2014.

Capici, Gaetano. *Bulldozer*. Ann Arbor, Mich.: Cherry Lake, 2011.

Schuh, Mari. *Bulldozers*. North Mankato, Minn.: Amicus, 2018.

Websites

Kikki's Workshop
http://www.kenkenkikki.jp/e_index.html
Explore this site to learn more about construction equipment.

SoftSchools.com: History of the Bulldozer
http://www.softschools.com/inventions/history/bulldozer_history/355/
Read more about how modern bulldozers were made.

Note: Every effort has been made to ensure that the websites listed above are suitable for children, that they have educational value, and that they contain no inappropriate material. However, because of the nature of the Internet, it is impossible to guarantee that these sites will remain active indefinitely or that their contents will not be altered.